"Jennie's book reminds us that while most millennials do not live in a pastoral fairy-tale lily pad, it is always better to approach our 21st-Century problems like timeless, whimsical, clothed amphibians: with humor, honesty, and with a generous dose of kindness toward others and ourselves."

—**Felipe Torres Medina, writer for**
The Late Show with Stephen Colbert

"I laughed, I cried, I felt hopeful and mad and tired and seen. But mostly I felt jealous because who writes this well all the time?"

—**Brooke Preston, co-author of**
***New Erotica for Feminists* and co-founder of The Belladonna**

"From dealing with crappy Wi-Fi to wanting everyone to like you, this modern take on a truly great classic had us laughing out loud. We've never related more to our favorite amphibian duo! *Frog and Toad Are Doing Their Best* is just the laugh we need these days."

—**Laura Lane and Ellen Haun, authors of**
Cinderella and the Glass Ceiling: And Other Feminist Fairy Tales

"This book will be famous, so I'm glad my name is on it."

—**Elissa Bassist, editor of**
the Funny Women column on The Rumpus

FROG AND TOAD
ARE DOING THEIR BEST

Bedtime Stories for Trying Times

A PARODY

by Jennie Egerdie
Illustrated by Ellie Hajdu

RUNNING PRESS
PHILADELPHIA

Running Press
Hachette Book Group
1290 Avenue of the Americas, New York, NY 10104
www.runningpress.com
@Running_Press

Printed in the United States of America

First Edition: October 2021

Published by Running Press, an imprint of Perseus Books, LLC, a subsidiary of Hachette Book Group, Inc. The Running Press name and logo is a trademark of the Hachette Book Group.

The Hachette Speakers Bureau provides a wide range of authors for speaking events. To find out more, go to www.hachettespeakersbureau.com or call (866) 376-6591.

The publisher is not responsible for websites (or their content) that are not owned by the publisher.

Print book cover and interior design by Frances J. Soo Ping Chow.

Library of Congress Control Number: 2021934656

ISBNs: 978-0-7624-7846-0 (hardcover), 978-0-7624-7847-7 (ebook)

LSC-H

Printing 3, 2022

To you,

for the good times,

the bad times,

and the in-between.

CONTENTS

AUTHOR'S NOTE

A wise man once said, "To be an adult is to be a little sad all the time."

That man was me, stress eating inside my small apartment during the worst year on record. When I wasn't panicking, I'd escape my reality by envisioning a gentler world. A kinder world. A world inhabited by talking animals.

That world came to me through Arnold Lobel's classic Frog and Toad stories, a series about enduring, loving friendship. I pictured Frog and Toad struggling with familiar frustrations—like wrestling with the Wi-Fi router or worrying about money—with the same humor, compassion, and occasional grumpiness as in the original books. Through Frog and Toad, I began to see my own challenges as temporary. Insignificant moments in my life became grand adventures. I see myself in Frog and Toad and I hope you do, too.

So, grab a cup of tea, a blanket, and settle in for a bedtime story tailor-made for you. Because, these days, adults need bedtime stories, too.

TECHNOLOGY IS HARD FOR FROG AND TOAD

Work from Home

Toad woke up.

In his bed was last night's dinner plate.

And last night's water glass.

And last week's pile of laundry.

"Drat!" Toad said to himself. "This room is a mess."

Frog opened the door.

"Oh," said Frog, "so this is where all our dishes are."

"I will clean up later," said Toad. "It is time for work."

Toad changed into his work pajamas.

He reached under a pillow for his laptop and opened his email.

"I have so much work to do," sighed Toad.

He set his Zoom background to a picture of his room when it was tidy.

"There," said Toad. "Now I am ready for the day."

Wi-Fi

Toad was writing an email.

Suddenly, the Wi-Fi disconnected.

Toad restarted his computer.

The Wi-Fi still was not working.

"Frog," Toad yelled to the other room. "The Wi-Fi is not working."

"That is strange," Frog called back. "It is working for me."

Toad checked his Wi-Fi settings.

"It says the signal is fine," he yelled. "But it is lying."

Toad went to the router.

He unplugged it and plugged it back in.

"Now, router," said Toad. "Start working."

Toad waited.

The lights on the router blinked on.

The Wi-Fi was still not working.

Toad restarted the router again.

"Now, router," said Toad. "Start working."

The lights blinked on.

The Wi-Fi was still not working.

Toad shook the router.

"NOW, ROUTER!" yelled Toad. "START WORKING!"

Frog ran into the room.

"Why are you yelling?" he asked.

"This router is terrible," cried Toad. "It will not connect to my computer!"

"Maybe try moving your computer closer to the router?" said Frog. "But please stop shouting. I am trying to work."

Frog left the room.

Toad looked at the router.

He moved his computer closer.

He tried to connect to the internet.

He kicked the router.

"You are my nemesis," said Toad.

"What was that?" called Frog.

"Nothing," said Toad.

Computers

Frog and Toad sat inside the house at their computers.

"We have been sitting all day," said Frog.

"Yes," said Toad.

"We should go outside," suggested Frog.

"Absolutely," agreed Toad.

Frog and Toad sat at their computers.

An hour passed.

"We should go outside," said Frog.

"In a minute," said Toad.

The Fitbit

Frog was walking in circles around the house.

Toad looked up from his book.

"Frog," said Toad, "what on earth are you doing?"

"It is my Fitbit," said Frog. "I did not make my step goal yesterday, so I am trying to make up for it today."

Frog marched by, lifting his knees high.

"Frog," said Toad. "It is okay to miss a day."

"I feel guilty," puffed Frog. "I know it is healthy to get steps, so it must be extra healthy to get extra steps."

Frog began jogging around the house.

He ran faster and faster.

"Frog," said Toad, "slow down."

"One second!" yelled Frog.

He sped through the living room.

"You are making me dizzy!" shouted Toad.

"Hold on!" panted Frog. "I . . . have . . . to . . . get . . . the . . . ste—oops!"

Fwoosh! Frog slipped on a rug.

Thump! He fell on his back.

"Ow," said Frog.

Toad came running over.

He pulled Frog up to sit.

"Frog," said Toad, "I think that Fitbit is bad for your health."

"Toad," said Frog, catching his breath, "you have a Fitbit. How do you keep from getting carried away?"

"Easy," said Toad. "I keep mine in a drawer."

Packages

The doorbell rang.

Toad opened the door and found a package.

"Frog," said Toad. "I think our new toaster has arrived."

"Oh, good!" called Frog.

Toad unpacked the toaster.

He took the empty box to the garage.

Inside, the garage was overflowing with empty boxes.

Boxes on the floor. Boxes on the car.

Boxes on top of boxes.

Toad threw the box onto the nearest pile and quickly closed the door.

"Whew," said Toad. "We order a lot online."

"The garage belongs to the boxes now," said Frog.

The Meal

Toad sat near the pond, reading on his phone.

Frog walked by.

"Hello, Toad," said Frog.

Toad did not say anything.

"Toad?" said Frog. "Can you hear me?"

Frog nudged Toad with his foot.

Toad looked up, startled.

"Oh! Hello, Frog," said Toad. "I did not hear you."

"What are you looking up?" said Frog.

"Places to eat," grumbled Toad. "I am hungry. But I cannot decide where to go."

"Maybe we could go somewhere together," said Frog.

"Good idea," said Toad.

"I will look up some options," said Frog.

"Me, too," said Toad.

Frog and Toad looked at their phones.

They looked at their phones for a long time.

A cloud drifted slowly above the pond.

"We could get Italian food," said Toad, "or split a big plate of nachos."

"What about pizza?" said Frog.

Frog and Toad looked at their phones.

The wind blew the reeds back and forth.

Their stomachs growled.

"How about burgers?" said Toad.

"I had a burger for lunch," sighed Frog.

Toad stomped his feet in frustration.

"I do not care what we eat!" cried Toad. "We need to make a decision!"

A crow swooped down.

"Excuse me," said the crow. "Are you lost?"

"No," Toad croaked miserably. "We are trying to decide where to eat."

"How about Subway?" suggested the crow.

Toad hid his face in his hands and moaned loudly.

"He does not mean to be rude," explained Frog. "He just really dislikes Subway."

The crow shrugged and flew away.

Toad felt his stomach rumble.

"Frog," said Toad, "I am very hungry. And my phone is about to die."

"Mine, too," said Frog. "What if we go home and have leftover spaghetti?"

"Sounds great," said Toad. "And we can charge our phones."

FROG AND TOAD FEEL VULNERABLE TODAY

The Dark

In the middle of the night, Toad woke up from
a nightmare.

He was being chased through a forest by a red-tailed
hawk who wanted to sauté him with a pat of butter
on his YouTube cooking channel.

It was very scary.

"Frog," whispered Toad. "Frog, are you there?"

There was no answer.

"Frog," Toad whispered a little louder.

He heard a creak in the floorboards.

Toad hid his head under the covers.

He stuck his hand out and reached for a book on his
bedside table.

He threw the book against the wall. *Thwap!*

It made a very loud noise.

Toad listened from under the blanket.

At first, all was quiet.

Then he heard loud footsteps approaching his door.

Suddenly, the lights turned on.

Toad peeked out from under his blanket.

A very groggy Frog stood in his doorway.

"Toad," said Frog.

"I'm sorry," said Toad.

"You could have come and got me," Frog pointed
out crossly.

"I was scared," said Toad.

"Of the dark?" said Frog.

"Yes," said Toad.

Toad hid under the covers.

Frog sat on the bed.

"It is all right to be afraid of the dark," said Frog.

"No, it is not," said Toad, his voice muffled by the pillow
he was squeezing. "I am grown."

"So?" said Frog.

"I know, rationally, there is nothing scary in the
dark," reasoned Toad. "But at night, sometimes, I still
get scared."

"We all get scared," said Frog. "I am scared of
the closet."

"You are?" said Toad.

"I must sleep with the closet door open," said Frog.

"Why?" said Toad.

"To see if any monsters are coming," said Frog.

"Good sense," said Toad.

Frog went to the kitchen and brought back a glass of water.

"The water at night is special," said Frog, offering the glass to Toad. "It makes you extra brave and will help you go back to sleep."

Toad smiled and rolled his eyes.

He drank all the water.

"Thank you, Frog," said Toad, snuggling under the covers.

Frog turned off the light.

"Next time, do not throw a book at the wall," said Frog.

"No promises," yawned Toad.

The Portrait

One rainy day in spring, Frog asked Toad if he could
paint his picture.

"You paint?" exclaimed Toad. "I never knew!"

"It is my new hobby," said Frog proudly. "I want to paint
a handsome portrait of you to hang over our fireplace."

Toad was flattered.

"Will you pose for the painting?" asked Frog.

"Of course!" said Toad. "How is this?"

Toad stood with one foot on the kitchen stool, gazing into the distance.

"That is a nice pose," said Frog, "but it does not capture your essence."

"Okay," said Toad, "how about this?"

Toad jumped in the air, his arms and legs spread wide like a star.

"That is very good," said Frog, "but it must be a pose you can hold for a while."

"Got it," said Toad.

Toad ran to the bookshelf.

He stood hugging all his favorite books.

"Perfect," said Frog. "Hold still."

Toad stayed very still while Frog painted.

He imagined how beautiful the painting would be.

Frog is so good at everything, Toad thought to himself. *I'll bet the painting will be amazing.*

After a while, Frog laid down his paintbrush.

He looked miserable.

"Oh, no," said Toad. "Did I move too much?"

"No," said Frog, shaking his head. "I am not good at painting."

"May I see?" asked Toad.

"No, no," said Frog, grimacing. "It is terrible."

"Let me look," insisted Toad.

Frog showed Toad the painting.

Toad inspected it from every angle.

He didn't say anything for a long time.

"It is wonderful," declared Toad.

"It looks nothing like you!" cried Frog.

"That does not matter," said Toad. "What matters
is how it makes me feel."

Toad placed the painting on the mantel over
the fireplace.

"Your painting makes me feel warm," said Toad.

Frog looked at the painting.

He inspected it from every angle.

He didn't say anything for a long time.

"It looks . . ." said Frog. "It looks the way you make
me feel."

"Exactly," said Toad.

They stayed there, staring at the painting, feeling
very warm together.

The Selfie

Toad and Frog went for a long walk.

They walked across a large meadow.

They walked in the woods.

They walked along the river.

They stopped to take a selfie.

"Smile!" said Frog.

"I am too tired to smile," grumbled Toad. "This walk

is long. My muscles are not what they used to be."

Frog looked at the photo.

"I do not like how I look," said Frog. "I am old

and ugly."

"You are not old or ugly," said Toad. "You are

beautiful."

"I look round," sighed Frog.

Toad stared at Frog.

It was his most intense stare.

"Round is a beautiful shape," said Toad.

Frog smiled.

Hat Store

On Toad's birthday, Frog gave him a hat.

Toad was delighted.

"Happy birthday," said Frog.

"Thank you, Frog! It is just my style," said Toad.

Toad put on the hat to take a photo for Frogstagram.

The hat fell down over his eyes.

"Oh, no," said Frog. "That hat is much too big for you.

Don't worry. I have a gift receipt."

Frog and Toad walked to the hat store.

They were greeted by a very dapper rat.

"Welcome to Hat Planet," said the rat. "The number-
one bonnet boutique. How may I help you?"

"I would like to exchange this hat for a smaller size,"
said Frog.

"I'm sorry," said the rat. "We're sold out."

"Drat," said Toad.

"But take a look around," offered the rat. "You can
exchange this for any other hat in the store."

Frog and Toad looked at their options.

They looked at newsboy hats.

They looked at straw hats.

They looked at warm woolen toques for the winter.

Then, suddenly, Toad pointed at a hat.

"That one!" said Toad. "I must try on that one!"

Frog turned a pale light green.

"Ah, yes, a fedora," said the rat. "Excellent choice."

Toad placed the fedora on his head.

"Frog," said Toad. "What do you think?"

Frog swallowed very hard.

"Toad," said Frog. "I know it is your birthday. But you are my best friend, and I cannot lie to you. That hat is terrible."

"Really?" said Toad.

"You look good in anything," said Frog. "Except for that hat. That hat is very, very bad."

"What if I wear it like this?" asked Toad.

He cocked the hat at a jaunty angle.

"That is worse," said Frog. "That makes you look like a men's rights activist."

Toad looked in the mirror.

He looked at himself hard.

"Oh, no," said Toad. "You are right."

"I am sorry," said Frog.

"No," said Toad, taking off the hat. "Thank you for telling me."

"Friends do not let friends dress like internet trolls," said Frog.

Toad turned to the sales rat.

"Can we order a different size of the hat my friend bought me?" asked Toad.

"Absolutely," said the rat. "And because it is your birthday, I will throw in free express shipping."

"Thank you," said Toad.

When Toad woke up the next morning, his birthday hat had arrived.

It was just the right size.

"Frog, Frog!" Toad cried. "This hat is perfect. Thank you."

To celebrate, Frog and Toad ate leftover birthday cake for breakfast and posted a video on ToadTok.

"Frog," said Toad, "someday, when I am old, I may wear a fedora."

"When you are old," said Frog, "It will look wonderful on you."

Smiling

Frog and Toad were walking home.

Every time they passed a stranger, Toad smiled and waved.

Sometimes the stranger smiled back.

Mostly, no one seemed to notice.

"Whew!" said Toad, rubbing his cheeks. "Smiling is hard work!"

"You do not have to smile," said Frog.

"I know," said Toad. "I smile because I need everyone to like me."

"Everyone?" asked Frog.

Toad nodded. "It is exhausting."

"Toad," said Frog. "How do you know they do not like you?"

Toad stopped in his tracks.

"I do not know," said Toad slowly.

"What if," said Frog, "they are not thinking about you at all?"

"Oh," said Toad, his eyes wide in disbelief. "That would be very good."

Frog reached over and squeezed Toad's hand.

"If it helps," said Frog, "I like you the best."

"That does help," said Toad.

"Maybe, if you think about that," said Frog, "you will not need everyone to like you."

At that moment, a field mouse walked down the street.

"Give it a try," said Frog. "Practice on him!"

"All right," said Toad.

The mouse came closer.

"Remember," whispered Frog, "you do not care if he likes you."

Toad narrowed his eyes with focused firmness.

The mouse was very close now.

Toad held his breath.

He leveled his eyes to meet the mouse's passing gaze.

Then he smiled and waved furiously.

The mouse looked confused and walked away quickly.

"I thought you did not need everyone to like you anymore," said Frog, exasperated.

"I do not need it," said Toad. "But I want it very much."

The Dance

One evening, Toad and Frog took a walk by the river.
On the bank, a small crowd had gathered around a
weasel with a boom box playing salsa music.

"Free dance class!" the weasel called warmly. "Beginners
welcome!"

Frog turned to Toad, excited.

"What luck! It is just starting!" exclaimed Frog.

Toad looked nervous.

31

"I do not know how to dance," said Toad.

"The weasel will teach us," said Frog, reassuringly "It will be like *Dirty Dancing!*"

". . . I love *Dirty Dancing*," admitted Toad.

"Everybody does," said Frog.

Frog and Toad found spots behind two fireflies swirling gracefully.

"Welcome, welcome!" said the rhythmically writhing weasel. "We'll start with a basic salsa step. It's left foot forward, step, back! Right foot back, step, forward. See?

"What did he say?" said Toad.

Frog did not hear him. He was too focused on the steps. Toad tried to follow, but his feet kept getting tangled.

"Frog," Toad whispered loudly. "Does this look right?"

"Good!" called the weasel to the crowd. "Now try it to music!"

"Wait—" said Toad.

A trio of boisterous salamanders bopped in unison. Frog wiggled his shoulders neatly in time. A garter snake slithered sensually, slapping her tail to the beat.

Toad was utterly confused.

"One-two," said Toad, as he hopped from foot to foot.

"One-two-three—"

"Wonderful!" yelled the weasel, spinning in step. "Now, on the three, add a turn!"

"Oh, no, no, no," said Toad.

He stopped dancing.

As Frog spun, he saw Toad standing still.

"What is wrong, Toad?" asked Frog.

"I cannot do it," said Toad. "I cannot salsa. It is all too much."

Toad's heart was racing.

His eyes started to fill with tears.

"I am here, Toad," said Frog. "Take some deep breaths."

Frog rubbed Toad's back.

He did not stop until Toad felt calm.

"Thank you, Frog." said Toad. "I am sorry I got so anxious. I forgot to take my Lexapro today."

"Do not be sorry!" said Frog. "Besides, who cares if you cannot follow the steps? We should just dance how we want!"

"But everyone is salsa-ing," said Toad. "We will look goofy."

"So what?" said Frog.

Frog and Toad listened to the music.

Toad started to shimmy.

And shake.

And jump.

Frog waved his arms in the hair and kicked his legs to the music.

Toad started whooping.

He forgot all about counting steps.

He twirled in circles.

Frog spun him around.

"THAT'S THE SPIRIT, AMPHIBIANS IN THE BACK!" yelled the weasel.

Frog and Toad ignored the instructions.

They danced wildly.

They were filled with joy.

FROG AND TOAD
HAVE DEBT

Bank Account

Toad stood in front of an ATM.

He took a deep breath.

Toad put his card into the machine.

"Hello," read the ATM. "Please enter your PIN."

"Blah," said Toad.

He entered his birthday.

The machine beeped.

"Please try again," read the ATM.

"Um . . ." said Toad.

He entered Frog's birthday.

The machine beeped again.

"One try remaining," read the ATM.

Toad's brow furrowed.

"Four digits," muttered Toad. "Four digits, four

digits . . . wait!"

Toad typed in 8623.

The ATM screen blinked its approval.

Of course, thought Toad. *8623 spells Toad, and I am Toad.*

"Checking or Savings?" read the ATM.

Toad took a nervous pause.

He clicked Savings.

"Your balance," read the ATM, "is $16."

"Phew," said Toad. "It is all in there."

New Coat

In the window of a boutique was a beautiful blue jacket with bright brass buttons.

Toad stared in the window.

"Oh, Frog!" cried Toad. "What a nice jacket!"

"It would look great on you," said Frog. "You could use a new jacket."

Toad looked at his coat, worn out from many seasons of wear.

"I cannot afford a new coat," said Toad sadly. "Maybe I can fix up my old one?"

"Sure," said Frog. "Do you know how to do that?"

"No," said Toad. "But I will start right away."

Toad ran home, taking a shortcut through the tall grass.

He took his sewing box down from the shelf.

"This will be a snap," said Toad to himself.

The next few hours were incredibly frustrating.

Toad cut and sewed and patched and darned every inch of his coat.

He used every color of thread, every button, and every patch in his sewing kit.

He used two Tide to Go pens on an old soup stain on his lapel.

Finally, as the sun set, he was finished.

Toad put on his coat.

It felt a bit uncomfortable with all the changes.

He walked into the living room to show Frog.

"What do you think?" asked Toad.

"I think . . . ," said Frog, searching for words.

Toad looked in the mirror.

He saw how lumpy his stitching was.

He looked at the mismatched patches on the now too-tight sleeves.

He looked at the stubborn stain on his lapel.

He was very frustrated.

Toad jumped up and down and shouted, "I tried so hard! It still looks terrible!"

Toad ran to the bedroom and slammed the door.

He got into bed, pulled the covers over his head, and fell asleep.

The next day, Frog made Toad a special breakfast.

Then, Frog took Toad back to the store.

They looked in the window at the beautiful jacket.

"Toad," said Frog. "Do you want this jacket?"

"Yes," said Toad.

"Do you need this jacket?" asked Frog.

Toad looked at his old coat.

He tugged at the tight, uncomfortable sleeves.

He looked at the stain on his lapel.

"Well . . . ," said Toad. "Maybe."

"It is okay to buy something for yourself," said Frog.

"But I have debt," said Toad.

"That does not mean you can't have nice things,"
said Frog.

Frog nudged Toad toward the store.

Toad went in and bought the jacket.

When he came out, Toad jumped for joy.

It fit perfectly.

He knew that coat would last him a long time.

Lottery

Toad scratched off a lottery ticket.

"Frog, Frog!" cried Toad.

Frog came running into the room.

"What is it, Toad?" said Frog.

"I won $5 dollars in the lottery!" said Toad.

"That is wonderful," said Frog.

"Yes," beamed Toad. "And it is only my first one!"

Toad pointed to a huge pile of scratch-off lottery tickets

spread out on the table.

Frog turned pale.

"Toad," said Frog, "that is a huge waste of money."

"Not at this rate!" said Toad. "I already made a
$3 profit!"

"Is there any way you can return some of these?"
asked Frog.

"Why would I?" said Toad. "I am going to be
a millionaire!"

Toad scratched off another ticket.

"Blah. I lost," said Toad, tossing the ticket on
the floor. "Oh, well!"

"Toad," said Frog, using his most serious voice.

"The odds of winning the lottery are so slim—"

Toad gave Frog a look.

It was his most annoyed look.

"Frog," said Toad. "Let me enjoy this."

"I can do that," said Frog.

Toad scratched off another ticket.

"WINNER!" yelled Toad. "Two more dollars for Toad!"

"Congratulations," said Frog. "You must be very lucky."

The Restaurant

Toad and Frog stood outside a lavish French bistro.

Inside, a caterpillar, two dragonflies, and a field mouse were having dinner together.

They looked like they were having a good time.

"We should treat ourselves to supper!" said Toad.

"What a good idea," said Frog.

Frog and Toad read the menu.

It was very expensive.

"Unless," offered Frog, "there is something you do not like about this place—"

"No, no," said Toad. "It looks great."

Toad and Frog did not move.

"This will be fun," said Toad.

"So much fun," said Frog.

Frog and Toad stood very still.

Neither one reached for the door.

The silence was tense.

"Then again," said Frog, "fancy food can be so . . ."

"Yes," said Toad, relieved. "I was about to say the same thing."

"I never know how to order wine," said Frog.

"I never understand why it costs so much for such small portions," said Toad.

Frog and Toad walked around the corner to a local diner, run by a friendly raccoon.

They split a giant sandwich, some nachos, and a thick slice of strawberry cake.

"Now this is a treat," said Frog, patting his very full belly.

"Yes," said Toad. "Luxury is a state of mind."

Mail

Frog came outside to check the mail.

Toad was sitting on the curb next to the mailbox.

"What are you doing, Toad?" asked Frog.

"I am waiting," said Toad, "for the tax refund."

"We already got our tax refund," said Frog.

"I know," said Toad. "But it was not enough. I am

waiting for another one."

"What would you do with it?" said Frog.

"I would pay off my credit card debt and get an eye exam," said Toad. "How about you, Frog?"

"I would spend some on groceries and save the rest for the mortgage payment," said Frog.

"Oh," said Toad. "Right. The mortgage payment."

Toad looked worried.

Frog sat on the curb with Toad.

"Another tax refund would be good," said Toad.

"Yes," agreed Frog. "As long as we don't owe anything!"

Frog laughed.

Toad did not laugh.

They sat there all afternoon, waiting together.

FROG AND TOAD PRACTICE SELF-CARE

Plans

By 9:30 on Saturday morning, Frog had already finished his morning workout, read the newspaper, and written a to-do list for the day.

"Toad! Toad!" said Frog. "It is time to start the day!"

"Blah," said a voice from the living room.

On the couch was a Toad-shaped pile of blankets.

"Toad?" asked Frog.

"Who is Toad?" said the voice. "No one here but us blankets."

Frog pulled the blankets from the couch.

Underneath was Toad, his eyes glued to his tablet.

"Argh!" said Toad, blinking furiously. "It is cold! And bright! I do not like it!"

"I have planned our day!" said Frog.

"Frog, it is Saturday," grumbled Toad. "This is what I am doing today."

Frog ignored Toad.

"First, we will walk through the meadow to greet the morning," said Frog. "Next, we will cook a recipe we have never tried before. Then, at one o'clock—"

"All that in one morning?" winced Toad.

Toad pulled the blanket over his head.

"But, Toad," cried Frog, "from two to four o'clock we will do a puzzle! And organize the garage!"

"Toad is not here right now," mumbled Toad.

Frog sat next to Toad, feeling disappointed.

After a few moments, Frog went to the kitchen.

He poured a hot cup of coffee.

He placed the coffee in front of Toad.

Toad sniffed.

He snuffed.

He peeked his head out of the blanket.

"Is this for me?" asked Toad.

"Yes," said Frog. "Can we start over?"

Toad took a sip of coffee.

"Yes, please," said Toad. "I am a little grumpy. I was up all night watching *Designing Swimmin'*."

"What is that?" inquired Frog.

"It is a sitcom," Toad said, brightening. "About these

newts who design ponds. The boss is the best, Julia Sugarlizard. She is a cold-blooded amphibian with a red-hot temper."

"Would you like me to watch with you?" said Frog.

Toad took another sip of coffee.

"How about," said Toad, "we watch one episode now, and then do one thing from your list?"

"That," said Frog, "is a great plan."

Frog and Toad drank coffee on the couch.

They watched the show.

Then they went outside to spend the day together.

Cookies

Toad pulled cookies out of the oven.

He set them on a rack to cool.

Frog came into the kitchen, sniffing.

"Those cookies smell very good," said Frog.

Toad took a bite.

"Frog, Frog," cried Toad, "taste these cookies!"

Frog ate one of the cookies.

"These are the best cookies I have ever eaten!" said Frog.

Frog and Toad ate many cookies, one after another.

"You know, Toad," said Frog, "I think we should

stop eating—"

Toad held up his hand.

"Not another word," said Toad, with his mouth full.

"This week has been hard enough."

"You are right," agreed Frog, reaching for

another cookie.

Frog and Toad ate all of the cookies.

Once they were done, they lay down for an

afternoon nap.

It was the best day.

Sheet Masks

Frog and Toad carefully placed sheet masks on
their faces.

"Now what?" said Toad.

"Now we relax," said Frog. "Let the masks soak in and
make us beautiful."

Frog lay down on the couch.

He closed his eyes and hummed a soothing tune.

It sounded like Enya.

Toad looked in the mirror.

A strange, Toad-shaped face mask stared back.

"Oh," said Toad. "I look like a serial killer."

Toad tiptoed over to the couch.

He bulged out his eyes and put his face very close
to Frog's.

"Hello, Frog," said Toad in a deep, creepy voice.

Frog opened his eyes and chuckled.

"You do look a bit scary," said Frog.

"Freaky Frog and Spooky Toad," said Toad.

"Boo!" said Frog.

"Aiee!" yelled Toad, laughing.

Frog smoothed the mask over his face.

"We must sit still," said Frog. "If we keep talking,
we

will wrinkle the masks and they will not work."

"That is okay," said Toad, peeling off his mask.

"Laughing makes me beautiful."

Bird-Watching

Frog and Toad were sitting outside. Frog was writing in a notebook.

"What are you doing, Frog?" said Toad.

"I am watching birds," said Frog. "And logging what I see in my birding journal."

"I like to watch birds," said Toad.

"It is very nice," said Frog. "Join me."

Frog and Toad looked out into the front yard.

They watched a cardinal fly by.

"That is one," said Frog, scribbling.

They saw a blue jay on her way to the park.

"There is another," said Toad.

They observed their new neighbor, a chickadee, drag a lawn mower out of their garage.

"That is three," said Frog, writing in his journal.

Toad waved hello.

He watched as the chickadee mowed his lawn.

"Frog," asked Toad, "Do birds go bird-watching?"

"I do not know," shrugged Frog.

"Maybe they watch us," suggested Toad.

Frog lowered his binoculars slowly.

"I never thought of that," said Frog.

Frog and Toad sat in silence, thinking.

After a long time, Toad spoke.

"Frog, I like watching birds. I do not mind if they watch us."

"Me, neither," said Frog, lifting his binoculars again.

"It only seems fair."

The Calendar

Frog looked at Toad's calendar.

The April page was on top.

"Toad," said Frog, "do you think it is still April?"

"No," said Toad, "I know it is August. But my brain feels stuck in April, so I leave it up."

"I understand that," said Frog.

Frog stared at the dates.

He thought about how each square represented a day gone by.

"Toad," said Frog, "the older I get, the less I understand time."

"Time means nothing," said Toad. "Time is just the thing that happens between snacks."

News

Toad sat on the front porch reading.

He looked very miserable.

Frog came outside.

"What is wrong, Toad?" asked Frog.

"This is my least favorite time of day," said Toad. "It is the time I read the news."

"Oh," said Frog.

"It makes me very unhappy," said Toad.

"Why is that?" asked Frog.

"What do you mean?" scowled Toad. "Do you not read the news?"

"I do," said Frog. "But I try not to take it in emotionally."

"What!" cried Toad, incensed. "How is that possible?! There is so much pain in the world!"

"The news makes me very scared," said Frog.

"So?" yelled Toad. "Everyone is scared! And hurting! And I have no idea how to stop it!"

"I can only handle so much!" yelled Frog.

Frog and Toad stood on the porch in silence.

They were very upset.

Just then, the snail mail carrier came to deliver the mail.

He crawled by very slowly.

It took him a while to reach their mailbox.

"Hello, Frog and Toad," said the snail. "Sorry for the wait. The mailbag is heavy today."

"Do you want some help?" called Frog.

"Oh, that would be very nice," the snail said, then added hastily, "but only if you have some free time."

"Of course," said Toad, forgetting his anger. "It would be no bother."

Frog carried the mailbag.

Toad helped hand over the letters.

In a short time, all the mail was delivered.

The snail was grateful.

He thanked Frog and Toad warmly, then inched away to spend the day with his family.

"What are you smiling at, Frog?" said Toad.

"I am happy we could help," said Frog.

Frog and Toad walked together, looking at the trees.

When they reach home, Toad put away the news.

It turned out to be a very pleasant day after all.

HOLIDAYS ARE HECTIC
FOR FROG AND TOAD

Fireworks

On the Fourth of July, Toad found a note on the
kitchen table.

The note said:

> *Dear Toad,*
> *Today was bad. My boss yelled at me and I am afraid*
> *I will lose my job. I have gone for a walk to clear my head.*
> *I will meet you in the park to watch the fireworks.*

"Poor Frog," said Toad. "I will cheer him up."

Toad gathered two lawn chairs.

He grabbed a big bag of chips.

He made Frog's favorite gin cocktail and poured it into
a cold thermos.

This will be the best Fourth of July yet, thought Toad as he
hurried to the park to get a good spot.

While waiting for Frog, Toad watched others arrive
for the show.

A painted turtle and three hatchlings sat on a picnic blanket, playing with bubbles.

A group of teenage chipmunks chattered and giggled in an oak tree.

In the parking lot, a puffed-up bullfrog and his newt bros unloaded a flag-covered cooler.

They immediately started playing beer pong in the back of their truck.

Soon, the sun set.

A trio of young shrews twirled sparklers in the twilight.

But Frog had not arrived.

Toad tried calling Frog's cell phone, but it went straight to voice mail.

Frog always answers his phone, thought Toad. *Where is he?*

Toad stared into the darkening crowd.

All he saw were shapes in the night.

What if one of those shapes is Frog? Toad thought, worried about his friend. *He is already having a bad day. What if he cannot find me?*

Toad stood up.

"Frog!" he cried. "Frog! I am here! Frog!"

The turtle family stared at Toad.

The smallest hatchling laughed until her parent

shushed her.

Toad started jumping and yelling.

He took off his T-shirt and waved it like a flag.

"FROG!" cried Toad. "ARE YOU THERE? IT'S

ME, TOAD!"

A family of garter snakes slithered by.

"Pleasssse," hissed the snake prissily. "Put your ssshhhirt on, there are familiesss pressssent."

Toad ignored the prudish snake.

With his left hand, Toad waved his shirt. With his right hand, he turned the flashlight on his phone to make a spotlight.

He jumped and waved and wiggled his arms.

"FROG!" yelled Toad. "FROG! OVER HERE!"

"Yes, I know," said a voice behind him.

Toad spun around.

Frog stood there, smiling.

"Frog!" cried Toad. "I was worried that you'd miss the fireworks!"

"I was in such a bad mood, I almost did," said Frog.

"Are you feeling better?" asked Toad.

"Much," said Frog. "Thanks to you."

"Happy to be of service," said Toad.

Frog and Toad took their seats.

They ate the chips and drank the special gin cocktail.

Together, they watched and cheered as fireworks sparkled in the night sky.

Camping

On a long holiday weekend, Frog and Toad arrived at
a campsite.

Frog leapt out of the car.

"You are going to love camping," said Frog. "It is
so relaxing."

Toad stepped out of the car.

"Blah," said Toad. "This campsite looks like it is full
of ticks."

Frog handed Toad a sleeping bag.

He passed Toad two pillows.

He piled the tent into Toad's arms.

"I feel something on my leg!" cried Toad. "Is that a tick?"

"You are fine," said Frog. "That is just a blade of grass
tickling your leg. Now where do you want to set up
the tent?"

"Inside a Best Western?" suggested Toad.

Frog led Toad over to a spot under a leafy tree.

Frog set up the tent poles.

He attached the tent.

Toad stared down at his legs.

"Frog," said Toad, "are you sure this isn't a tick bite?"

"Yes, Toad," said Frog.

"I am afraid of ticks," said Toad.

"Do not be afraid," said Frog. "I will make sure no ticks bite you. Now, time for a fire!"

Frog placed the firewood by the fire pit.

Toad sat on the hood of the car.

"I will show you how to start a fire!" said Frog.

"In a minute," said Toad, staring at his phone. "I am searching for what a tick bite looks like."

Frog sighed.

"I am going to look for some kindling," said Frog. "Try to relax, please."

Toad stared at the quiet campsite.

He listened to the wind rustling through the leaves.

This is nice, thought Toad.

Toad unrolled his sleeping bag and lay down.

He stared at the blue sky.

I can see why Frog likes this, thought Toad. *It is peaceful.*

Then Toad fell asleep.

"Toad, Toad, wake up," said Frog. "Look at all the kindling I found!"

Toad looked up.

Frog stood there.

In his arms were bunches of twigs.

On his left leg was a bug.

"TICK!" screamed Toad.

Bang!

Toad threw his phone at Frog's leg.

Thud!

Frog dropped all the kindling on his toes.

Crash!

Toad ran headlong into the nearby tree.

"Ouch!" said Frog, hopping on one foot.

"Ow," said Toad, clutching his head.

Frog checked his leg.

"Toad," said Frog. "It was not a tick. It was a sunflower seed."

Toad shuddered.

"Frog," said Toad. "I think camping is too stressful for me."

"I see that," said Frog. "But where will we relax?"

"Where we do all our best relaxing," said Toad.

"At home."

Thanksgiving

The day before Thanksgiving, Frog and Toad read a
cookbook together.

"We should make these recipes for the holiday,"
said Toad.

"Do you think we are good enough at cooking?" said Frog.

Toad looked into Frog's eyes.

"We are excellent chefs," said Toad.

"Are we?" said Frog.

Frog and Toad picked up everything they needed from
the grocery store.

They went to the bakery and selected a pumpkin pie.

Then, on Thanksgiving morning, Toad took charge of
the kitchen.

"Frog, you will chop up the Brussels sprouts," instructed
Toad. "I will prep the potatoes."

"Yes, chef!" saluted Frog.

Toad put three pots of potatoes on the stove.

He put a few pats of butter in each pot.

"Butter is delicious," said Toad. "I am a fabulous chef."

Next, Toad lined a baking sheet.

"Ready for the sprouts!" said Toad.

"Not yet," said Frog.

Frog chopped the vegetables slowly and methodically.

"You have to go faster than that," said Toad.

"But the book says they must be evenly sliced," said Frog.

"Well, hurry up," Toad said impatiently. "We have not even started the main course."

Toad went to the freezer.

He pulled out a very small frozen turkey.

"That is supposed to be thawed by now, right?" asked Frog.

"I thought it would happen quickly," said Toad, unsure.

"What is that smell?" said Frog.

Toad sniffed.

"MY POTATOES ARE BURNING!" yelled Toad.

Toad ran to the stove.

In his haste, he knocked the turkey off the counter and onto Frog's foot.

"OUCH!" yelled Frog, hopping in pain. "That thing is frozen solid!"

"Oh, no," moaned Toad. "My potatoes are all singed."

"I need to sit down," said Frog.

"No!" wailed Toad. "We will never get this done!"

Frog grabbed ice from the freezer for his foot.

He surveyed the kitchen.

"Toad," said Frog, "I know you want to make these recipes. But what do we have right now that will be ready for suppertime?"

"Well . . ." said Toad, looking at all the mess in the kitchen. "We have the pie and your Brussels sprouts. And I suppose we have an emergency box of mac and cheese in the pantry."

"I think that would be a fine dinner," said Frog.

"Me, too," said Toad, relieved.

Frog put the turkey in the freezer for another holiday. Toad composted the burnt potatoes and saved the rest to make hash browns.

That night, they sat down for a feast of Brussels sprouts, pumpkin pie, and cheesy pasta.

It was, all things considered, a tasty meal.

"Frog," said Toad. "We may not be great cooks, but we are great company."

"Hear, hear," said Frog.

Black Friday

On the last Friday in November, Frog and Toad spent
the morning reading.

In the afternoon they raked leaves.

In the evening they watched TV.

"Today was Black Friday," said Frog.

"Oh," said Toad. "Did you need anything?"

"Not particularly," shrugged Frog. "I do not care about
Black Friday."

"I like that about you," said Toad.

Wrapping Presents

Frog and Toad came home from holiday shopping.

"These need to be mailed tomorrow," said Frog. "So we must wrap the presents today."

"I will do it!" offered Toad.

Toad went to the closet.

He pulled out scissors, ribbons, tape, and rolls of wrapping paper.

Frog's mother likes green best, thought Toad. *So I will wrap her present in sparkly green paper.*

Toad cut a crooked square.

"This piece is too small," said Toad.

Toad cut a much larger piece.

He folded paper over the gift.

Now there is too much paper, thought Toad. *No problem, I will tape the edge down.*

He pulled out a long stretch of tape.

He placed it over the folded paper.

He pulled another piece of tape.

Again and again, he taped the present.

He taped the sides.

The edges.

The front.

He taped and taped until the gift was a mass of crinkled paper coated in layers of tape.

"Oh, no," cried Toad. "It looks horrible!"

Toad grabbed the bright red ribbon.

He wound it over and over the gift until the crinkled, mashed paper was barely visible.

Then he tied the ribbon in a giant bow.

"Frog," called Toad. "Want to see your mother's present?"

Frog came into the room.

"Ta-da!" said Toad.

"Good heavens," said Frog. "I will wrap the others."

"Yes," said Toad. "That would be best."

Resolutions

On New Year's Eve, Frog set out champagne glasses. He
put an extra log on the fire.

Suddenly, Toad burst through the door.

"I have it!" said Toad.

"Happy New Year's Eve to you, too," said Frog.

"Yes, yes, Happy New Year," said Toad hastily. "I picked
my resolution!"

Toad kicked off his boots and hung up his coat, hat,
and scarf in the closet.

Frog waited for him by the fire.

"My New Year's resolution," said Toad as he flopped
down in his seat, "is to get really muscular this year."

"No," groaned Frog.

"Yes," said Toad. "I will work out and get very,
very muscly."

"That is a terrible idea," cautioned Frog.

"It will be great," Toad insisted. "Picture me with
great big muscles, all strong and bulging . . ."

Toad flexed his arms for effect.

Frog hid a smile.

"But you will have to buy new shirts," said Frog.

"That would be a pain," said Toad. "Maybe I will keep thinking. What is your resolution, Frog?"

"I am going to make more money," said Frog.

"How?" asked Toad.

Frog shrugged. "If I knew, I would have done it already."

"You made the same resolution last year," pointed out Toad.

"Yes," said Frog, "but I did not do it last year."

"That is the problem with resolutions," grumbled Toad. "It has to be something you will do."

They sat together quietly, imagining the new year. Outside, the moon rose over piles of snow. The logs crackled in the fire.

"I read," said Frog, "that the best resolutions are meaningful and realistic to achieve."

"But I am not sure what is realistic," said Toad. "I do not know what will happen next year."

"That makes it hard," agreed Frog.

"Wait," said Toad. "I have it."

"Is it meaningful?" asked Frog.

"Yes," said Toad.

"Is it realistic?" asked Frog.

"Yes," said Toad.

"And you can achieve it no matter what happens?"
asked Frog.

"Yes," said Toad.

"Well," said Frog, "what is it?"

"My resolution," said Toad, "is to spend the year
with you."

"That is a good one," said Frog.

As the snow outside sparkled to greet the winking stars,

Frog and Toad raised their glasses.

"To us," said Frog.

"Always," promised Toad.

They sat by the fire,

Warm and happy,

Waiting to meet another year together.

ACKNOWLEDGMENTS

This book would not exist without the kindness and generous support of my agent and friend Laura Mazer, Ellie Hajdu, Elissa Bassist, Caitlin Kunkel, Brooke Preston, Jess Riordan at Running Press, Chris Monks at McSweeney's Internet Tendency, and my fantastic first readers Sarah Garfinkel, Kerry Elson, Jenn Knott, and Audrey Burges—if you ever need a kidney, it's yours. (First come, first served.)

I would not exist without my amazing parents, Lisa and Mark, whose home is a haven of laughter and love. To my best friend/sister Molly and my lovely brother-in-law Dan, to Anna, Claire, Molly R. and Kyra, thank you for always taking my calls and for filling my life with joy.

Last and most importantly, to my partner Matt. Thank you for reading, for listening, and for always being the Frog to my Toad.

ABOUT THE AUTHOR

Jennie Egerdie is a writer, performer, and editor living in Brooklyn, NY. Most recently, her work appears in the humor anthology *Merciless & Unpredictable: A McSweeney's Guide to Parenting*. She is also a contributor to McSweeney's Internet Tendency, Weekly Humorist, The Belladonna, and many other publications. Visit www.jennie.fun for more humor and stories.

ABOUT THE ILLUSTRATOR

Ellie Hajdu is an illustrator and a toy designer for Folkmanis Puppets. Her work has been featured on *Saturday Night Live*, *Late Night with Seth Myers*, and *The Late Late Show with Craig Ferguson*, and in specialty toy and gift stores, science and nature museums, and other specialty retailers around the world. She lives in the San Francisco Bay Area, and you can find more of her work at elliehajdu.com and on Instagram at @elliehajdu.